GIFT TO THE
Academy of the Sacred Heart
Bloomfield Hills, Michigan

Donated by

The Libre Book
Club
February, 2009

Count On It!
Three

¡Cuenta con ello!
Tres

Dana Meachen Rau

Marshall Cavendish
Benchmark
New York

Three cats.

Tres gatos.

Three holes.

❖

Tres agujeros.

5

Three sides.

❖

Tres lados.

Three bowls.

❖

Tres tazones.

Three wheels.

Tres ruedas.

Three bags.

❖

Tres bolsas.

13

Three scoops.

❖

Tres bolas de helado.

Three flags.

———❖———

Tres banderas.

17

Three!

———❖———

¡Tres!

Words We Know
Palabras conocidas

bags
bolsas

bowls
tazones

cats
gatos

flags
banderas

20

holes
agujeros

scoops
bolas de helado

sides
lados

wheels
ruedas

21

Index

Índice

About the Author

Dana Meachen Rau is the author of many other titles in the Bookworms series, as well as other nonfiction and early reader books. She lives in Burlington, Connecticut, with her husband and two children.

Datos biográficos de la autora

Dana Meachen Rau es la autora de muchos libros de la serie Bookworms y de otros libros de no ficción y de lectura inicial. Vive en Burlington, Connecticut, con su esposo y dos hijos.

With thanks to the Reading Consultants:

Nanci Vargus, Ed.D., is an Assistant Professor of Elementary Education at the University of Indianapolis.

Beth Walker Gambro is an Adjunct Professor at the University of St. Francis in Joliet, Illinois.

Agradecemos a las asesoras de lectura:

Nanci Vargus, Dra. en Ed. y profesora auxiliar de Educación Primaria en la Universidad de Indianápolis.

Beth Walker Gambro, profesora adjunta en la Universidad de St. Francis en Joliet, Illinois.

Marshall Cavendish Benchmark
99 White Plains Road
Tarrytown, New York 10591
www.marshallcavendish.us

Library of Congress Cataloging-in-Publication Data

Rau, Dana Meachen, 1971–
[Three. Spanish & English]
Three / by Dana Meachen Rau = Tres / por Dana Meachen Rau.
p. cm. – (Bookworms. Count on it! = Bookworms. ¡Cuenta con ello!)
Includes index.
ISBN 978-0-7614-3475-7 (bilingual ed.) – ISBN 978-0-7614-3446-7 (Spanish ed.)
ISBN 978-0-7614-2968-5 (English ed.)
1. Three (The number)–Juvenile literature. 2. Number concept–Juvenile literature.
I. Title. II. Title: Tres. III. Series.
QA141.3.R27918 2009
513–dc22
2008017588

Editor: Christina Gardeski
Publisher: Michelle Bisson
Designer: Virginia Pope
Art Director: Anahid Hamparian

Spanish Translation and Text Composition by Victory Productions, Inc.
www.victoryprd.com

Photo Research by Anne Burns Images

The photographs in this book are used with permission and through the courtesy of:
Corbis: pp. 1, 11, 21BR Lawrence Manning; pp. 3, 20BL Alley Cat Productions; pp. 7, 21BL Bernard Kohlhas/zefa;
pp. 13R, 20TRR Lew Robertson; pp. 15, 21TR Steven Mark Needham/Envision; pp. 17, 20BR PictureNet.
SuperStock: pp. 5, 19, 21TL age fotostock; pp. 9, 20TR Nicholas Eveleigh; pp. 13L, 20TLL Photodisc.

Printed in Malaysia
1 3 5 6 4 2